Dear McAninch Family,

In memory of
County McAninch. We
are so sorry, for your
loss.

With Love,
The Lundstroms

LAST WILL AND TESTAMENT

OF AN

EXTREMELY DISTINGUISHED DOG

THE

LAST WILL AND TESTAMENT

OF AN

EXTREMELY DISTINGUISHED DOG

Eugene O'Neill

Illustrated by
ADRIENNE YORINKS

Henry Holt and Company ⅋ New York

For dogs . . . How desolate the world would be without you.

—A. Y.

Henry Holt and Company, LLC
Publishers since 1866
175 Fifth Avenue
New York, New York 10010
www.henryholt.com

Text reprinted with permission from the Yale Collection of American Literature,
the Beinecke Rare Book Manuscript Library, Yale University.
Illustrations copyright © 1999 by Adrienne Yorinks
All rights reserved.
Distributed in Canada by H. B. Fenn and Company Ltd.

Library of Congress Cataloging-in-Publication Data
O'Neill, Eugene, 1888–1953.
The last will and testament of an extremely distinguished dog /
Eugene O'Neill: with illustrations by Adrienne Yorinks.—1st ed.
p. cm.
ISBN-13: 978-0-8050-6170-3
ISBN-10: 0-8050-6170-3
1. Dogs—Fiction.   2. Pets—Death—Psychological aspects.
I. Yorinks, Adrienne.   II. Title.
PS3529.N5L29   1999   99-36351
813'.52—dc21   CIP

Henry Holt books are available for special promotions and
premiums. For details contact Director, Special Markets.

First Edition 1999

Designed by Kelly S. Too

All photographs by Arthur Yorinks except pages 15, 40–41 by Adrienne Yorinks
and page 35 by Helene Berg; quilts photographed by Karen Bell

Printed in China
17 19 20 18 16

FOREWORD

I first read *The Last Will and Testament of an Extremely Distinguished Dog* after receiving a copy in the mail from my friend Robert Moran a couple of weeks before Syd, my first dog, died. Bob knew how much Syd meant to me and was gracious and kind to have sent me this compact and compelling piece of writing.

For almost twelve years Syd was my best friend. I was completely devastated that the end of her life was so near, and it was impossible to imagine living without her. Nothing could console me. But when I read O'Neill's essay it lessened the pain of losing Syd. I felt hope that she could find her own paradise, a place where she no longer ached and suffered in a body that was betraying her.

I will always love Syd, and from reading O'Neill's heartfelt words I have come to realize that because of her I will never be without a dog in my life.

Many thanks to Eugene O'Neill for having written this beautiful essay and to Arthur Yorinks, for his love of dogs and for the immense help he gave to me on this book.

Adrienne Yorinks
North Salem, New York

I, Silverdene Emblem O'Neill (familiarly known to my family, friends, and acquaintances as Blemie), because the burden of my years and infirmities is heavy upon me, and I realize the end of my life is near, do hereby bury my last will and testament in the mind of my Master. He will not know it is there until after I am dead. Then, remembering me in his loneliness, he will suddenly know of this testament, and I ask him then to inscribe it as a memorial to me.

I have little in the way of material things to leave. Dogs are wiser than men. They do not set great store upon things. They do not waste their days hoarding property. They do not ruin their sleep worrying about how to keep the objects they have, and to obtain objects they have not.

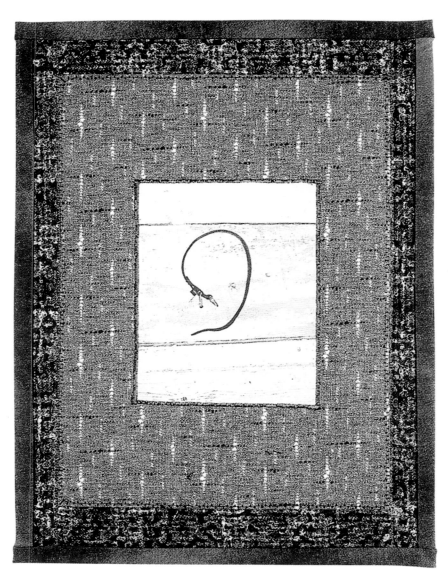

There is nothing of value I have to bequeath except my love and my faith. These I leave to all those who have loved me, especially to my Master and Mistress, who I know will mourn me the most.

I ask my Master and my Mistress to remember me always, but not to grieve for me too long. In my life I have tried to be a comfort to them in time of sorrow, and a reason for added joy in their happiness. It is painful for me to think that even in death I should cause them pain.

Let them remember that while no dog has ever had a happier life (and this I owe to their love and care for me), now that I have grown blind and deaf and lame, and even my sense of smell fails me so that a rabbit could be right under my nose and I might not know, my pride has sunk to a sick, bewildered humiliation. I feel life is taunting me with having overlingered my welcome. It is time I said good-bye, before I become too sick a burden on myself and on those who love me.

10

It will be a sorrow to leave them, but not a sorrow to die. Dogs do not fear death as men do. We accept it as part of life, not as something alien and terrible which destroys life. What may come after death, who knows?

I would like to believe that there is a Paradise. Where one is always young and full-bladdered.

Where all the day one dillies and dallies. Where each blissful hour is mealtime.

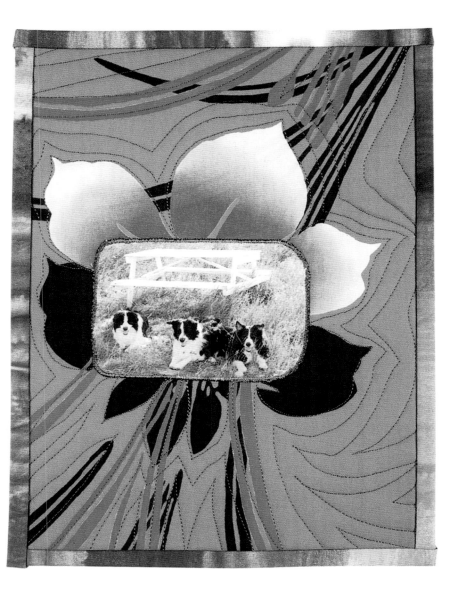

Where in long evenings there are a million fireplaces with logs forever burning, and one curls oneself up and blinks into the flames and nods and dreams, remembering the old brave days on earth and the love of one's Master and Mistress.

I am afraid this is too much for even such a dog as I am to expect. But peace, at least, is certain. Peace and long rest for weary old heart and head and limbs, and eternal sleep in the earth I have loved so well. Perhaps, after all, this is best.

One last request I earnestly make. I have heard my Mistress say, "When Blemie dies we must never have another dog. I love him so much I could never love another one."

Now I would ask her, for love of me, to have another. It would be a poor tribute to my memory never to have a dog again.

What I would like to feel is that, having once had me in the family, now she cannot live without a dog!

I have never had a narrow, jealous spirit. I have always held that most dogs are good.

My successor can hardly be as well bred or as well mannered or as distinguished and handsome as I was in my prime. My Master and Mistress must not ask the impossible.

But he will do his best, I am sure, and even his inevitable defects will help by comparison to keep my memory green.

To him I bequeath my collar and leash and my overcoat and raincoat. He can never wear them with the distinction I did, all eyes fixed on me in admiration; but again I am sure he will do his utmost not to appear a mere gauche provincial dog.

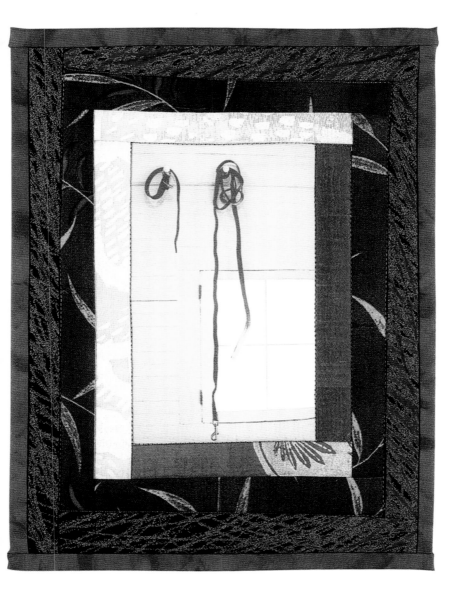

Here on the ranch, he may prove himself quite worthy of comparison, in some respects. He will, I presume, come closer to jackrabbits than I have been able to in recent years. And, for all his faults, I hereby wish him the happiness I know will be his in my old home.

One last work of farewell, dear Master and Mistress.

Whenever you visit my grave, say to yourselves with regret but also with happiness in your hearts at the remembrance of my long, happy life with you: "Here lies one who loved us and whom we loved."

BLEMIE

No matter how deep my sleep I shall hear you,
and not all the power of death

can keep my spirit
from wagging a grateful tail.